better together*

* This book is best read together, grownup and kid.

a kids
book
about

a

kids

book

about

REAL ESTATE
DEVELOPMENT

by Anyeley Hallová

A Kids Co.
Editor Emma Wolf
Designer Rick DeLucco
Creative Director Rick DeLucco
Studio Manager Kenya Feldes
Sales Director Melanie Wilkins
Head of Books Jennifer Goldstein
CEO and Founder Jelani Memory

DK
Delhi Technical Team Bimlesh Tiwary Pushpak Tyagi, Rakesh Kumar
Senior Production Editor Jennifer Murray
Senior Production Controller Louise Minihane
Senior Acquisitions Editor Katy Flint
Acquisitions Project Editor Sara Forster
Managing Art Editor Vicky Short
Managing Director, Licensing Mark Searle

First American edition, 2025
Published in the United States by DK Publishing, 1745 Broadway, 20th Floor,
New York, NY 10019

First published in Great Britain in 2025 by
Dorling Kindersley Limited, 20 Vauxhall Bridge Road, London SW1V 2SA
A Penguin Random House Company

The authorised representative in the EEA is
Dorling Kindersley Verlag GmbH. Arnulfstr. 124, 80636 Munich, Germany

A catalog record for this book is available from the Library of Congress.
A CIP catalogue record for this book is available from the British Library.
ISBN: 978-0-5939-7038-6

DK books are available at special discounts when purchased in bulk for sales
promotions, premiums, fund-raising, or education use. For details, contact:
DK Publishing Special Markets, 1745 Broadway, 20th Floor, New York, NY 10019
SpecialSales@dk.com

Printed and bound in China
www.dk.com
akidsco.com

MIX
Paper | Supporting
responsible forestry
FSC™ C018179

This book was made with Forest
Stewardship Council™ certified
paper – one small step in DK's
commitment to a sustainable future.
Learn more at www.dk.com/uk/
information/sustainability

This book is dedicated to all the inquisitive, creative, and bright kids who question how the world works and dream of how to make it a better place for people, animals, and plants.

Intro
for grownups

People often mistake me for an architect, builder, or real estate agent. Most folks don't understand what real estate development is. I am often sought out by women, people of color, and young adults who are passionate about environmental and social sustainability, seeking advice on how to enter the profession and build wealth through real estate.

If it's hard for grownups to understand real estate development, how can kids aspire to this profession? Historically, in the United States, land ownership, development know-how, and the ability to create wealth through real estate was exclusionary. This has created a big gap in knowledge and access to the power of real estate.

This book is designed to help kids and their grownups understand real estate development, and to inspire a diverse group of young people to become changemakers in their community.

Real estate development is

What do you see when
you look out your window?

Do you see office buildings?

Apartments?

A restaurant?

An industrial building?

Have you ever wondered...

How did it get there?

Who built it?

Why **is it there?**

Hi! My name is Anyeley.

And I'm a real estate developer.

WHAT DO I DO?

My job is kind of like being
the director of a MOVIE but
for building projects.

It's up to me to **envision a project** and put together a team of people to help design, build, and manage it.

(Like assistant directors, managers, or actors in a movie!)

Some of those people include...

ENGINEERS, ARCHITECTS, CONSTRUCTION WORKERS, PROPERTY MANAGERS, BROKERS, AND REAL ESTATE AGENTS.

I think through each step (or "scene") of the process and make sure the right people are involved in each decision.

And I need to know enough about each person's job to **empower them** to be the best they can be.

REAL ESTATE DEVELOPMENT is using money to buy a piece of land and build something on it, or buy an existing building and renovate it.

People who give their money to these projects are **investors**.

Investors can be individuals, groups of people, governments, or foundations.

I am an investor, too!

My job is to manage an investor's money (also called their **investment**).

When projects are built (and if they do well), investors get their money back and make even more money when they collect rent or sell the building.

That money, called a **return**, looks different depending on who invests.

And the return often isn't just money!

It can look like...

AFFORDABLE HOUSING
FOR COMMUNITY MEMBERS,

SPACES TO GROW
SMALL BUSINESSES,

A TREATMENT CENTER
FOR CLIENTS,

OR A COMMUNITY CENTER
FOR LOCAL ARTISTS.

Real estate developers **improve land** using financial support from others.

And those who invest want to see **value added** to the land that real estate developers improve upon.

Did you know any of that?

PROBABLY NOT!

And there are reasons why this information isn't super known.

IN THE UNITED STATES, the real estate development industry has historically been one of exclusion.

For a long time, land ownership was reserved for specific people.

Namely those who were white, male, and wealthy.

Land ownership matters because those who own land have the ability to choose what happens with that land and make money from it.

To develop, you may also need
to borrow money from a bank.

And this process *also* has
systemic barriers.

This means a few different things...

ONE, people outside of this exclusive group don't typically know about real estate development.

TWO, if they do know about it, they don't feel welcome to participate.

Or, they didn't know how to get the skills, because they never saw people who look like them in the industry.

AND LASTLY,
this underrepresentation leads to decision-making in communities of color or low-income communities which don't include the people who live in those neighborhoods.

AND THAT'S

NOT FAIR.

BUT IT DOESN'T HAVE TO BE THAT WAY.

I love what I do because I get to imagine ways for more people from different backgrounds to get involved in this industry.

Going back to the MOVIE idea,
I have to tell you a secret...

Real estate developers have often been the **bad guys** of the story.

FOR REAL!

WHY IS THAT?

Real estate development
has a lot to do with **money**.

And when money is the **ONLY**
priority, people who live in those
communities and the surrounding
environment get harmed.

Real estate is a risky business because investors can lose their money.

And a lot of people believe that including environmental and social aspects in development projects adds risk.

But to me, not including those pieces is *more* risky because we need healthy people and a healthy planet in order for our projects to work.

When people think of real estate development, they don't always think of...

SOCIAL JUSTICE, FIGHTING CLIMATE CHANGE, OR HELPING OTHERS.

But that's what I love about what I do.

When I daydream about the "City of the Future", I see...

Affordable Housing:
Everyone has a place to live and they can spend less of their money on rent.

LEED-Certified Green Building:
A healthy and energy-efficient building with solar panels that produce electricity for when the power goes out.

Community Building:
It serves and empowers the community through economic development and community services. This project is built by women- and people-of-color-owned businesses.

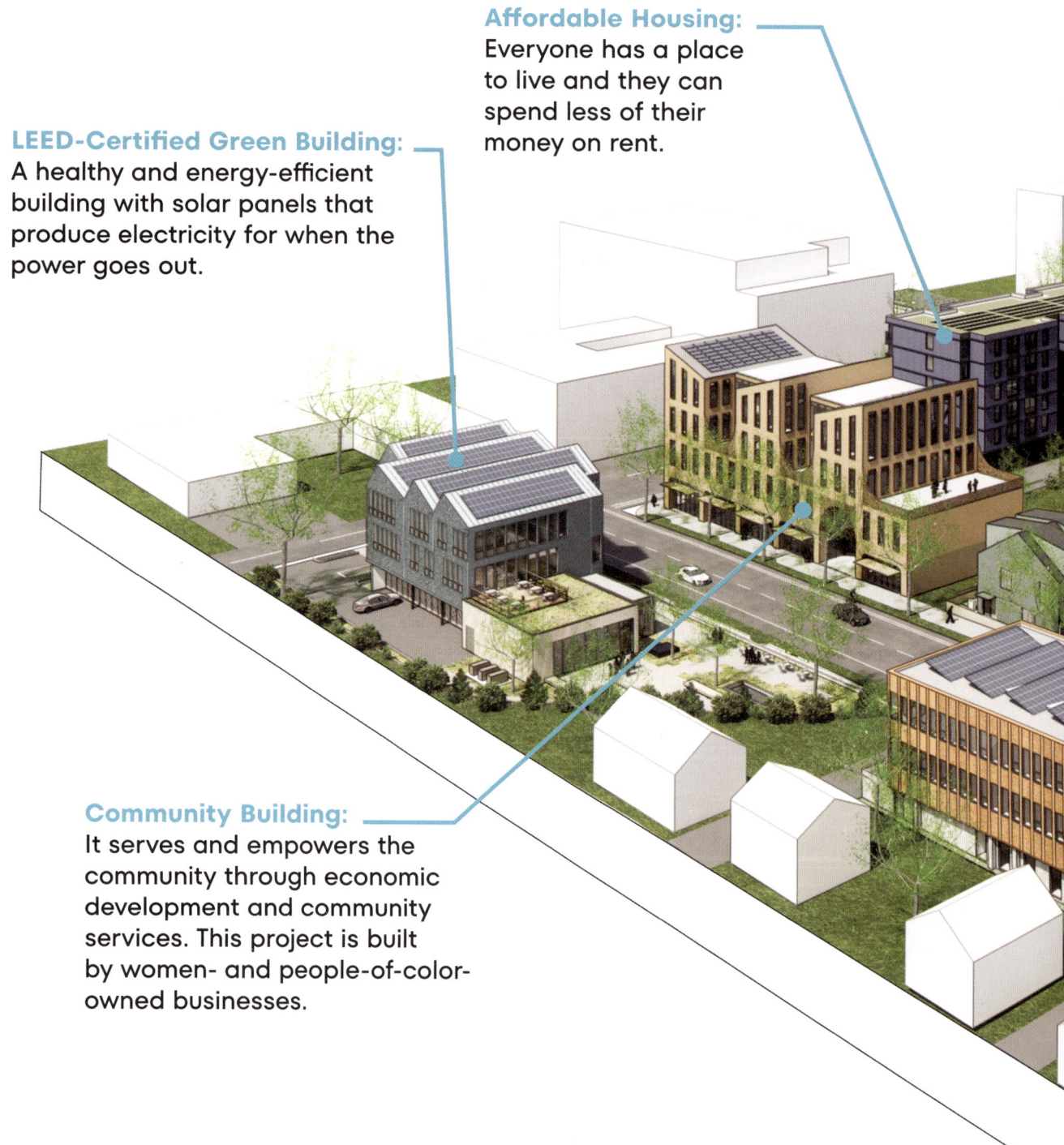

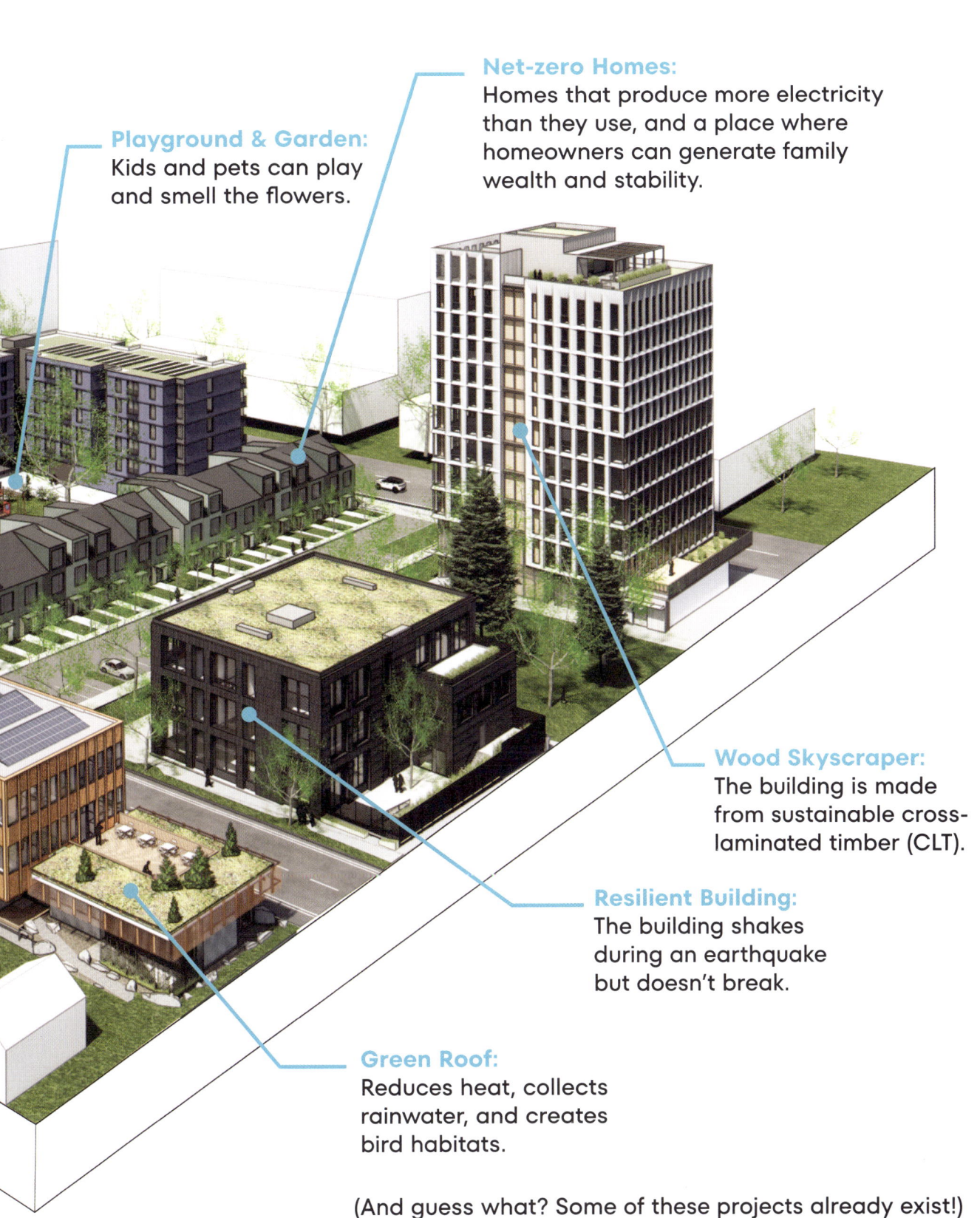

Playground & Garden:
Kids and pets can play
and smell the flowers.

Net-zero Homes:
Homes that produce more electricity
than they use, and a place where
homeowners can generate family
wealth and stability.

Wood Skyscraper:
The building is made
from sustainable cross-
laminated timber (CLT).

Resilient Building:
The building shakes
during an earthquake
but doesn't break.

Green Roof:
Reduces heat, collects
rainwater, and creates
bird habitats.

(And guess what? Some of these projects already exist!)

And we need more people
who care about these things.

PEOPLE JUST LIKE

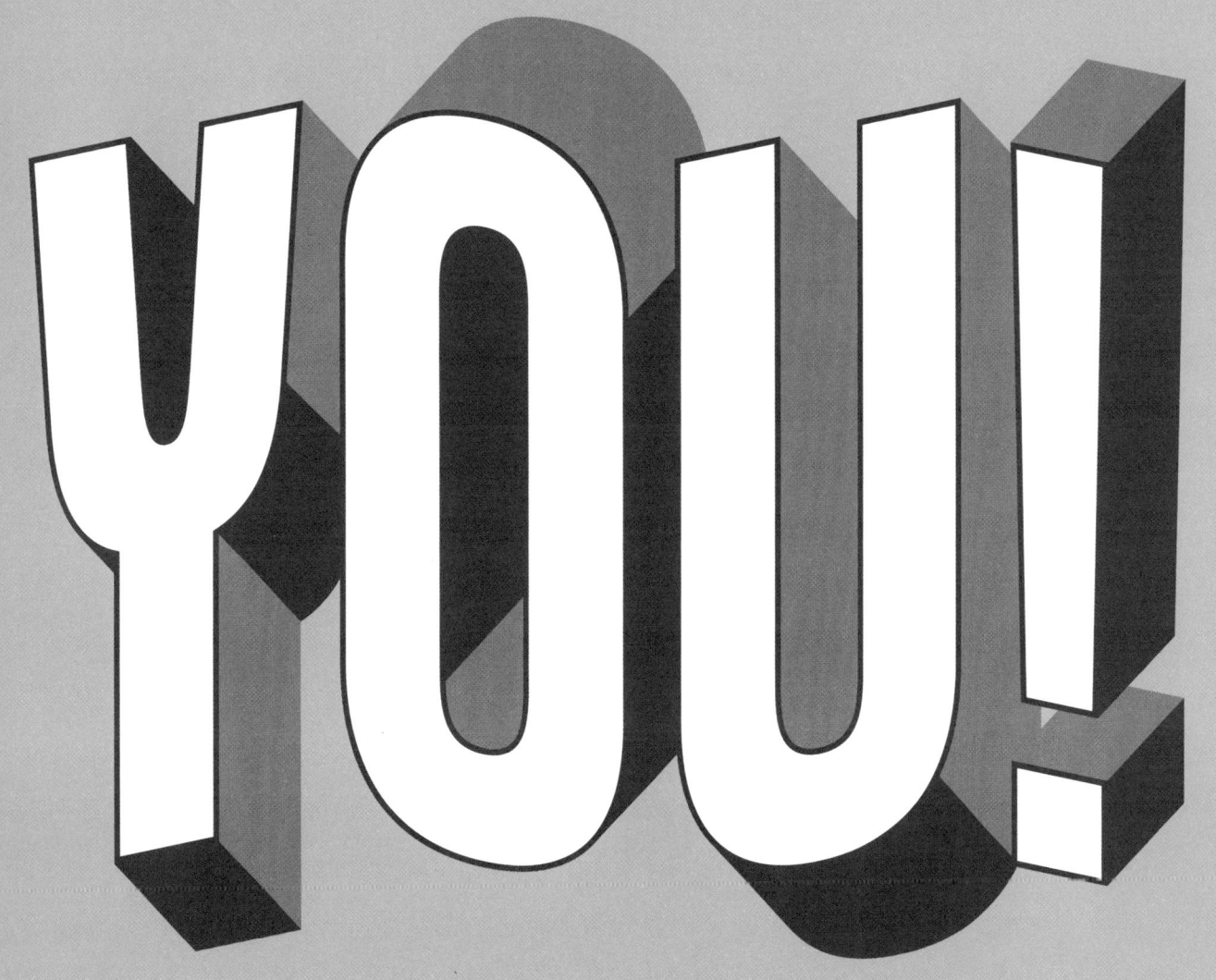

It's possible to get into real estate development through so many routes.

You can study pretty much any field, but a lot of people get into this industry through:

FINANCE,
BUSINESS,
PROPERTY MANAGEMENT,
CITY PLANNING,
ACTIVISM,
OR ARCHITECTURE.

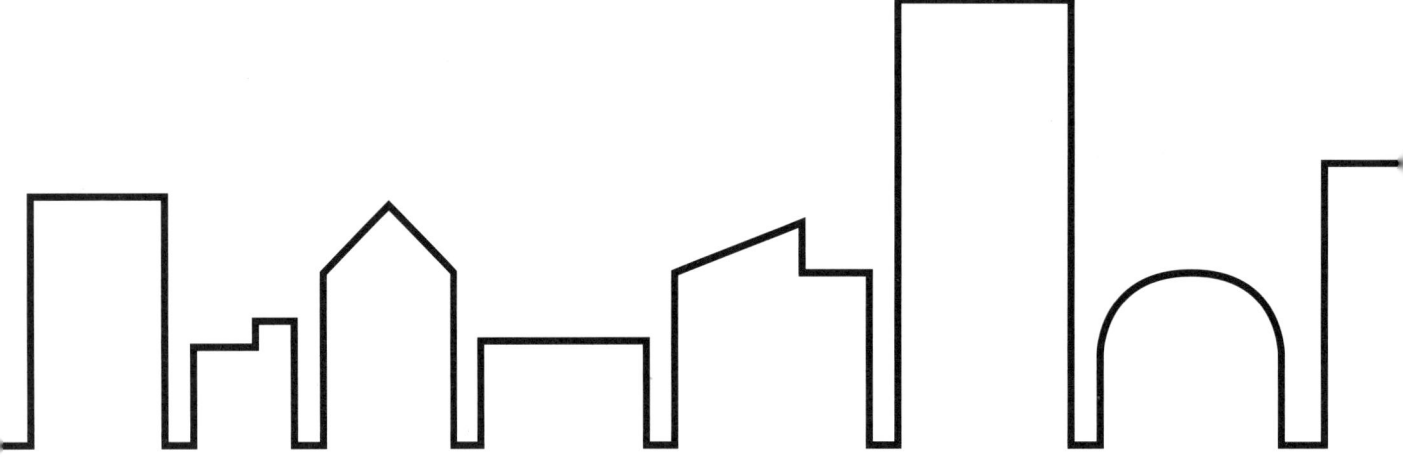

I went to school to study
city planning, but most of
what I learned about real estate
development came from working!

HERE'S THE TRUTH:

ANYONE
REAL ESTATE

CAN BE A DEVELOPER!

But if that doesn't sound like the job you want, you can still participate in real estate development in your community.

You can **share your vision** and priorities for your community with local officials.

You can **join in on workshops** about future development in your neighborhood.

You can **use your voice** in city council meetings.

Stand up for projects you support and care about.

YOUR VOICE MATTERS.

With more people like us
shaping the real estate around us,

IS BRIGHT.

Outro
for grownups

Now that you better understand real estate development, how will you and your kid continue to learn and be an active participant in real estate in your community?

In some areas, developers are required to seek input from nearby residents, providing an opportunity for community members to attend and share their priorities. Public projects like libraries or schools often ask for feedback during development and offer kid-friendly activities. Consider visiting open houses or taking tours of completed buildings. Modern home tours are my personal favorite!

Industry and community organizations now offer workshops and programs to introduce kids to development and related fields. Since real estate relies on financing, gaining financial literacy is crucial for both kids and grownups. Understanding budgeting, investing, saving, taxes, and insurance will enhance your understanding of real estate development and provide additional benefits when making real estate investment choices.

About The Author

Anyeley Hallová (she/her) wrote this book for any kid who notices changes in their neighborhood—like a vacant lot becoming an apartment building—and is curious about who or what made that happen.

When Anyeley was a kid, she loved touring model homes with her mom but had no idea who was behind making those developments come to life, or that she could be that person one day. Today, she lives her dream of developing innovative sustainable buildings that create wealth in communities of color.

This book is a tell-all for kids (and grownups) to push back the curtain on real estate development and get a sneak peek into her vision for the "City of the Future".

 @anyeleyhallova   @anyeley   @adre.dev   @adre

Made to empower.

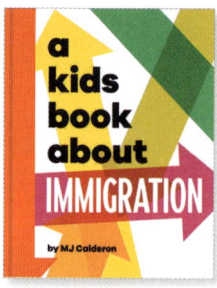

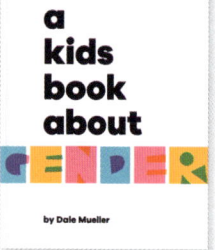

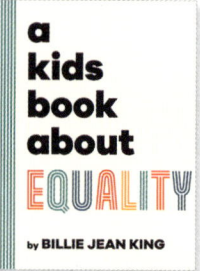

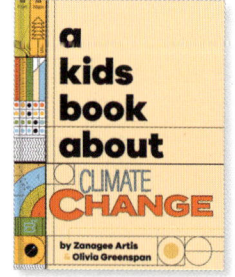

Discover more at akidsco.com